A Linen Crow, A Caftan Magpie

A LINEN CROW, A CAFTAN MAGPIE

PATRICK LANE

THISTLEDOWN PRESS

Canadian Cataloguing in Publication Data

Lane, Patrick, 1939-
        A linen crow, a caftan magpie

Poems.
ISBN 0-920066-94-1 (bound)
ISBN 0-920066-95-X (paperback)

I. Title.
PS8523.A53L55 1985   C811'.54   C85-091062-5
PR9199.3.L36L5 1985

Book design by A.M. Forrie
Cover painting by Louise Walters
Typesetting by Résistance Graphics, Edmonton
Set in 11 point Oracle

Printed and bound in Canada by
Hignell Printing Limited, Winnipeg

Thistledown Press
668 East Place
Saskatoon, Sask.
S7J 2Z5

For Lorna

Kasasagi no
Wataseru hashi ni
Oku shimo no
Shiroki wo mireba
Yo zo fukenikeru

Yakamochi
718-785

We remember minutely and precisely
all those things that did not happen to us.

Eric Hoffer

Remember the heart. Fog on the still river. First frost.
Passion. Flowers. The love of cities in old windows.

The painting is a dead eye. A window goes nowhere.
This one is alive. This one has a chance to live. This one.

Look in or out. Beauty is starved and love is afraid.
Dead children. The night in mothers. Remembered delight.

The heart is an argument with darkness. Moon sliver.
Dead eye. The room rings. I do not answer it again.

I love you. Your nakedness is between doom and heresy.
Do not mourn. The dried flowers do not need the sun.

The desire for cages. Who built this denial?
Art.

Zodiacs. The books of the dead. A magpie in snow.
There are no deceits. There are only lies.

Evening and I remember you. You and you are gone.
The origin of the lost poem. A window of words.

Magpie, magpie, do not take a lower branch than this.
Last home I dreamed I was night. Poverty and song.

Autumn. The crabapple drops its small and bitter fruit.
The old attend to their gardens. Under the earth. Love.

The ones who are lost sing longer than the ones who are alone.
Blind at birth, I want you back.

Stay with me, carrion bird.
I am thinking of last leaves. The beauty of beginning.

The line is doubtful. The meaning is clear. Endure.
We remember a boy in wind, a bell in an open field.

Full moon, I love you, your rising and your falling.
The cedar wax-wings are drunk. Frost on the berries.

Give of your grace. The sun forgives.
I am afraid of nothing. Blow wind. The bell is lonely.

The new world. The anvil. Water in deep well.
Between your hips the only parasite is me.

I tried to imagine a linen crow, a caftan magpie.
I believe I believe.

The love of the naive. That awkward integrity.
Searching for complaint, complaining.

She holds the needle but sews no stitch in time.
Undo the night.

Blue lines.
I know too many things. Everything broken.

I crave the honey yet complain of life. Be vivid. Be.
Exclude me. I am not fit to govern. Dictator. Maggot.

Parallel lines are relentless.
Quiet men. I make no sense of this.

And the world is not this, is this and not that.
Forty-five years.

Refusal.
Give me nothing. A caftan crow, a linen magpie.

Going to the lost and found.
Remembering precisely, minutely, the record of illusions.

Cornstalks. The wind holds the crow.
The broken leans away from everything.

I am eating a wild thing. Young heart. Divine wind.
And the river will freeze on time.

First snow on moving water.
The soft pain strikes. Spare me.

The mole's cry as he sleeps. Velvet death.
We rest in desolation, the mind creeping.

Remember the ridiculous.
The lenient master starves beauty.

Desolate. Desolate. The day and the day and the day.
Remember the heart. Little mole.

Last leaves. First frost.
I am the awaking. Your long cry of love.

Salamander searches for me. He wants to die.
The fire will not burn without symmetry.

There is no road without you.
Only the way can describe the lost. Little serpent.

Kept in a bamboo cage.
The only purpose is to stay alive.

I have designs on you. Intricate scrolls.
And the salamander burns with great beauty.

The throttle of pigeons in winter. Eave song.
Now we are anyone. This coming to love.

Our eyes. See. See. The myriad.
Crazed gold like insects. Waiting.

Mad images. Secular despair.
Dreams of pages. It is too cold for night.

When did I look out the window last?
Reproach. Flight in the leaves. First snow.

The free lance falls where it wills.
Subdue the flesh. Bury yourself in nothing.

The plains are a mind thinking slowly.
Art at war with itself. Make my mind go slow.

The sparrow's shoulders hunch in cold.
Ritual prolonged by rules. Games in stone. Go.

Clean your beak. Arrange your feathers.
The full stomach will not find God.

We did not leave the garden. We were left.
Bewildered. Forsaken.

And you, sweet enemy.
How you left us to die and die.

The snake has only one skin. Take it off.
When she eats you she does not ask your name.

Keep your apples and roses.
East of Eden, the only desert is the mind. Thinking.

A bad line, breaking wrong, hurts the eye.
How much worse the ear?

A mouth in a tree cries forgive, forgive.
Like a body fallen on a bed. A white bed. A body.

Forgive me.
I was going nowhere and going anyway.

The eyes that name you have no tongue.
Old roads. The arrival in time. Witnesses.

Life slides from the bone cage.
Only the rare eagle, the coyote, the enemy called man.

The answer to the answer. The wind knows where.
Eat the soft shell of the womb. Stormy waters.

The horizon turns to your eye.
Relief. It is this moment she remembers.

Wet sack on snow. Birth, you are a winter away.
Binding. She sings her seed to stand. Come, follow me.

Who will explain the bones?
The porcupine challenges your passing.

West of the west is the last thing you want.
Old sailor. Meet me again when I am hungry.

Step aside. Politeness has nothing to do with it.
The doe breaks through to clear water.

Words come slowly. Or not at all. Old buck hides.
Goshun painted the young willows. This way. Now!

The wild first of things, genital, weaving.
Sleeping my belly loves the sky. My back the earth.

My friends, we have fought too long with desire.
Give up artifice.

This line and that. Nothing more.
Love. Power. Virtue.

Be content. The dog who pisses leaves his memory there.
Yours is a time of order. The genital no.

Sturm und Drang, blut und broten.
Out of that voice. Broken syllables.

Rage in the heart.
The lost limb in the knot.

Dante's angels.
Spread your thighs. Anthologies of snow.

The cleft in the hill. Refugee from peace.
Let me give you the gift of the rose.

To make of nothing a tradition.
The pure.

The undisciplined think chaos order.
Fear and fragments.

Even the wolf's eye sees magpie's beak.
The anvil protests the hammer's dance.

Return.
The flower unfolds without you.

All that is left. Last names. Morning.
Blood ties. Saturn's breakfast.

He said.
The dead. I don't know why I'm alive.

The body also moves, incomparable, describing peace.
We have forgotten how to be strangers.

Parables smaller than a story.
Keep me awake. Let the blood sing. Last names. Morning.

Let the women have it. Empty tombs.
I grow wings. Outcast at last.

The living end of death. Faith in flowers.
The withered root. Without love, let it go.

So I have held you and holding, hold myself.
Beyond narcissism. Famine and death.

Little nuthatch, you hang in cold, busy.
I wear my words among strangers. Trust no one. Keep it.

Alien. These words remind me. Art. Sutras.
Hard as a diamond.

Essence.
Old prison. Welcome.

The puzzle of the empty cup. Eggs and onions.
A bird circles after long labour.

The beautiful is kept intact by the master.
Which of me is the slave?

An egg will not float in open water.
Life clusters on the margins. Marsh grass. Look out!

So you don't want a saint.
Enough of old men climbing mountains to drink tea.

The bird flies back for birth.
Teach me the stars. The way to summer.

Hesitant. The hidden languages.
You aren't going to trick me. Not this fool.

Love again. A dictionary of symbols.
Your body in the night is blue ivory.

A key. A knife. A stone.
Crows. Greed kills when you are young. Go hungry.

Fly me to the ruins. This is love. Runed.
Mockery. Meaning.

Rip out my tongue. My mouth can't mind.
Hold me. Hold me. Inside I am still young.

O let the last bird fly.
The way is made for him. White rushes.

Or leaving.
Full of doubt, this absence holds me.

Without love, let it go.
The shadows of the last geese cross my mind.

This holds me. Small beaks.
Shadows in the bark of old trees. Wings.

Don't shake your hoary locks at me. I am still hungry.
Laughter. How the mind works, works, works.

Widow-maker.
Charm-breaker.

Too many questions.
This is what is meant by noise. Tell me! Tell me!

Then turn, good friend.
These are your stars. The slivered moon rising.

Watching you watching is better than watching.
The lacquered mirror. You say concubine, wanting.

You have never. Go deep. Go deep.
Bring me roses. Polished stones. White roses and stones.

I want to swallow you. Fill my mouth with you.
One-eyed Jack. Wild one.

This place of tired guitars.
Broken lines. The flesh.

Women walk to the sea. Prosperous and obedient.
Their sweet indignity. Happy among stones.

Everything is island. Symbol of failure and hope.
Violence, they say, as if the word could ruin them.

Their prayer. A fish strangling on air. A drowned man.
Love or die. Or walk among gulls. The sea greets you.

Among stones. Caress yourself. The only thing is you.
This is the oldest song.

Go back.
In the old city a young city burns.

This life vanishes. We take it with us in a cup.
Flight.

Far to the south they are killing patience.
Perfectly. The horse with rubber heels is a heart.

Listen to the pavement. The beating of hooves.
They are coming. Lie down among stones.

First and last words. The memoirs of the moon.
My mouth between your legs. O flesh.

Each one of you greets me. Soft in the night.
My teeth in your shoulder. Laughing again and again.

A man in snow must wait for spring. Crystal night.
Blue light. Welcome wise one. Tell me a story.

Old hag.
Smell my flesh on your flesh when I am gone.

The snow does not know doubt.
Children laugh in their doorways. Take me!

This masque of night. This being no one.
The voluntary pain is exquisite. Voluptuary.

My theft. Stealing love till there's nothing left.
I want pain. Little pigeon.

In my eye. See.
Once I might have told you something. Mad woman.

The first pain of air.
Turtle-dance. Sweet water. Where are you?

Small. No one eat me while I run.
Death will not come. Will not. Come.

Big beak.
If you have only one leg, stand on it.

A jar full of rocks.
Tears, and nothing at the centre.

To remedy a bad world. Conquistador.
What we expect to see, we see.

Trust madness. There is nothing there.
The candle is out. Give yourself the light.

Do not think of these words.
Go in. There is no fault.

The battle is with form.
Rupture. Violence. Beyond the veil, astonishment.

Adorned. The weight of beauty. Willow leaves and almonds.
She decorates her world. But she sings alone.

Beauty. The patience of the dancer in the stone.
Still life.

The web in the garden. Little maker.
The moon hangs in a silver bag.

Meticulous craft. Immense time.
The correct wine has nothing to do with glass.

The natural man.
Fish a little. Hunt a little. Blow your head off.

You are naked when I find you.
There is grace in coyote's kill. He eats as well as he can.

As Buson said: *Pretty clever, eh?*
There is a bank on both sides of the river. Paddle fast!

Or take silence.
Ah, slow, slow. The alphabet began with the moon.

Pleasure. Success. Order.
Wisdom is laughter at the end.

The hardest to forgive is a friend.
Trust. Honour. As you go.

Don't be sorry. Art is short. Life is long.
Here. You pull the wagon.

Go. Move your mountain. Turn around.
Behind you is a mountain. Move it again.

I walk to the river in deep snow. The ice is thick.
In the heart of the city. Drunk and singing.

At least be happy.
Excellence in the small. Tears frozen on your face.

Lie with me here. We will make cold angels.
Dig inside words but don't hide your head there.

Why are you most happy when happiness fails?
Under the ice, fat fish, beaver, rat.

We end the near when we near the end. The particular moves.
All the crows fly south.

I make small moves toward love. In defence of nothing.
The artisan repeats the immortal like a slave.

So art does not labour.
I took my time. Here. Now you take it.

Memories are possessions. Don't hold on.
The argument with darkness. Dead reckoning. But magpie stays.

There are no last lines.
The trout in winter consumes himself. No waste.

The answer is not an answer. It refuses faith.
How we search for what is already known. Leaf. Stone.

Blood on my tongue.
But to rise with the wind. That ecstasy.

As the line moves. The leap!
Thrashing there.

Let me be stranger to your will.
The young persist. They swim in the old earth.

Assassin. Saint. Who wants paradise?
Fog on the river. The sun burns you away. Ice and magpies.

The geese in the south raise their heads in praise. Where now?
The blood remembers.

So I swim back to birth.
Old and old and old.

Patience.
Every battle of the warrior is with confused noise.

There are measures. They have weight. Great and small.
Rest now.

A linen crow. A caftan magpie. Sorrow and song.
The tree bends under its fruit.

The wait of time.
He who appears before you now is the toad of this thicket.

Acknowledgements:

A number of these poems were produced for CBC Radio by Wayne Schmaltz with original music by Tom Schudel and sung by Lori Erhardt. Others were published in *Canadian Literature* and *The South-East Asian Review*.

I wish to acknowledge Lorna Crozier, John Newlove, Sean Virgo, and Alice Van Wart, all of whom read through parts of the manuscript and gave me critical advice. The poems obey.

I would also like to thank The University of Alberta in Edmonton and The Library of Saskatoon where this sequence was completed. The residencies I spent there gave me the time to put some of my meditations in the form that appears here. That form is not the ghazal though I deluded myself for a time thinking it was. It is rather a composite of the haiku and ghazal, a resemblance and nothing more, perhaps more oriental than occidental. And finally to Isaiah, Schiller, Buson, and Basho, for their enlightenment.

The poem says it: *As the line moves. The leap!*
                  Thrashing there.

This book has been published with the assistance of The Canada Council and the Saskatchewan Arts Board.